TINY JUMPER

HOW TINY BROADWICK CREATED THE PARACHUTE RIP CORD

by Candy Dahl

illustrated by Maithili Joshi

little bee books

Georgia Ann Thompson weighed only
three pounds at birth on April 8th, 1893.

Everyone called her Tiny, and the nickname stuck.

For James, Finn, Luke, and Logan:
"Got a dream? No lollygagging. Go for it!"
—CD

To my mom, a fearless woman
who isn't afraid to jump.
She knows it'll be a soft landing.
—MJ

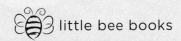 little bee books

New York, NY
Text copyright © 2023 by Candy Dahl
Illustrations copyright © 2023 by Maithili Joshi
Back matter photos courtesy of the State Archives of North Carolina.
All rights reserved, including the right of reproduction in whole or in part in any form.
Library of Congress Cataloging-in-Publication Data is available upon request.
ISBN 978-1-4998-1394-4 | First Edition | Manufactured in China   GGD 0423
2 4 6 8 10 9 7 5 3 1
littlebeebooks.com

For information about special discounts on bulk purchases,
please contact Little Bee Books at sales@littlebeebooks.com.

Since Tiny's family was poor, she had to start work when she was only six.

In one job, she STRETCHED

to pick caterpillars from tobacco leaves.

In another, she STRETCHED

to reach machine parts in a cotton mill.

The twelve-hour workdays exhausted Tiny.

She was tired of

loud noises

and coughing

and doing the
same task

over

and over.

After work, she would climb
to a treetop to get away from
everything and imagine rising

UP...

far away from fields
and mills.

Big dreams gave
her hope.

At the 1907 North Carolina State Fair,
she saw a way to make her big dreams come true.
She watched a hot-air balloon rise high, almost to the clouds,
with a man balancing on a trapeze underneath it.

The crowd gasped when the man
cut away from the balloon.

A silk parachute
floated him

S
L
O
W
L
Y
D
O
W
N

and back to earth.

This was how
she could rise up!

She marched right up to the
man and told him she must
be an aeronaut, too.

"When I saw that balloon go up,
and I gawked at it as it ascended
into the heavens, I knew
I'd never be the same."

World Famous Aeronuaut
Charles Broadwick
laughed at the idea
of such a tiny girl
having enough
guts to do what
he did.

But Tiny insisted
she was strong.

And brave.

Very brave.

She convinced Mr. Broadwick that a tiny, lively aeronaut
would draw people to his act, so he agreed to teach her.

Over the next year, Tiny learned
all about parachutes and hot-air balloons.
She studied the many aspects of wind and clouds.

At the 1908 State Fair, her determination paid off.

She waited to rise for her parachute jump.
Hot air slowly inflated the balloon.
Smoke filled Tiny's nose and burned her eyes.

But embarrassment
burned Tiny's face.

Mr. Broadwick insisted on making
Tiny seem much younger than fifteen.
He gave her the aeronaut name "The Doll Girl."

What would people
think of her wearing
ruffled bloomers
and a bonnet?
Ribbons and bows?

But Tiny was willing
to do whatever it took
to be an aeronaut.

"It burned me up having
to dress like a baby doll
and having that name
tacked on me!"

With the
huge balloon
fully inflated,
it began to lift.

UP
UP
UP

At two thousand feet,
the carnival tent
looked like a toy.

People seemed
no bigger than ants.

Tiny floated above the
tobacco field, above the mill.
Much higher than her
climbing tree.

The crack of a pistol shattered the silence—Tiny's signal to jump.

Her hands trembled as she cut her parachute away from the balloon.

She slowly
drifted

DOWN
DOWN
DOWN...

"I knew everything that I was
supposed to do, but nobody
told me that thrill that I was
going to get when I cut away
from the balloon."

. . . right into a blackberry bush!

When worried people rushed to save her,
Tiny smiled and popped a blackberry into her mouth.

Tiny became famous as she toured the country. Newspapers called her the most daring parachutist. Crowds gathered to see her jump from on high.

Tiny performed heart-stopping, triple parachute jumps.
She jumped at night with fiery flares.
She risked drowning when she landed in water.

Oftentimes, the wind blew her parachute off target.
Tiny landed in strange and dangerous places:

TRAINS

WINDMILLS

ROOFS

TREES

She broke her arms, shoulders, ankles, and feet.
But Tiny refused to stop doing what she loved best—

rising up into the sky.

"I had broken bones and dislocated
shoulders. I was young. I just kind of
grew up with it, and I loved it.
I loved the excitement."

By 1912, airplanes burst onto the public scene.
People lost interest in hot-air balloons.

Planes were new and exciting.
And dangerous.

Only the bravest adventurers would fly in them.

Double-dog daring Tiny told inventor Glenn Martin
she'd not only fly in his plane—
but she would even parachute from it!

No woman had ever parachuted from an airplane.

On June 21st, 1913, Tiny sat in a trap seat just outside of
a biplane zooming forward at eighty miles per hour.
The roar of the engine beat in her ears.
The wind whipped her face.

Tiny wore a coatpack that Charles Broadwick had invented.
Attached to the back of her canvas jacket was a pack that contained
a parachute. A long cable connected the pack to the plane.

When Mr. Martin raised his hand, Tiny released a lever.
Her seat disappeared, and she fell into nothingness.

The static line pulled taut and ripped open the pack's cover.

Tiny barreled through space, straight down, feet first...

The thin silk swished from the pack as Tiny hurtled even...

FASTER

FASTER

FASTER

FASTER

FASTER

FASTER

Finally, the parachute filled with air and jerked Tiny back.

She floated to the exact spot a huge crowd waited for her.

And landed
on her feet!

Tiny had become the first
woman ever to parachute
from an airplane!

"In a hot-air balloon, you had to travel the way the wind was taking you. The thrill
of knowing I could drop without having to look out for trees, telephone wires,
churches, and steeples—why, it was the nicest thing that ever happened to me!"

Interest in Tiny's airplane leaps spread across the country.
The United States Army Air Corps asked for a firsthand look,
so Tiny demonstrated the coatpack parachute to them
at San Diego's North Island.

Three times she jumped without a hitch.

But on the fourth jump, Tiny leapt from the plane
and immediately jerked to a stop.

Her parachute's line was tangled in the plane's tail!
Tiny twisted in midair as the plane zoomed forward.

She had dropped too far to climb back into the plane, but not far enough to rip away from the static line and open her parachute. The wind tossed Tiny left, right, and all around.

"When I got in the air, there was nobody that could help me, so I had to figure out the things that I could do to get back safely, without hurting myself or anybody else."

Tiny made a split-second decision.
She wrestled a knife from her
pocket and reached behind
her head. She sawed and
sawed at the line.

When the blade
severed the
last thread . . .

DOWN

Tiny dropped in a free fall,
air whistling past her ears.

DOWN

She plunged,
the hard earth
speeding toward her.

D
O
W
N

She shot at eighty feet per second,
clawing for the nub of line.

Tiny found it and jerked hard, breaking the strings that covered the parachute.

Six pounds of silk rushed

U P W A R D

and filled with air.

Tiny landed safely!

Tiny had become the first person ever
to make a deliberate free fall in a parachute.
The piece of line she pulled later became known as a rip cord.

The Army general proclaimed Tiny's demonstration
the most daring achievement he had ever seen!

"'You're a plucky girl,' said
the brigadier general.
'That's what they say, but I
call it joy. There's no real
fun except for up in the air.'"

In 1964 The Director of the National Air Museum stated that Tiny "stands tall among her colleagues—the pioneers of flight. And her contributions to flight history have helped to make America stand tall as the nation which gave wings to the world."

"They said back home that I'd get killed. They also said the Wright brothers couldn't fly, but I've lived to see all this advancement. I just hope I live until they get ladies on the moon, and I wish I were a little girl again because I would be among the first women to go to the moon."

Tiny's practical knowledge and top-notch skills helped advance the development and refinement of the pack parachute and rip cord.

These basic designs live on today.

People who jump from planes, civilian or military, use parachutes. They pull rip cords.

They float

D
O
W
N

to the earth
safely...

because a tiny woman with huge courage and determination followed her dreams of rising up into the sky and changed the world of parachuting forever.

AUTHOR'S NOTE

Georgia Ann Thompson, nicknamed Tiny, never reached five feet in height or weighed more than eighty pounds. At the age of fifteen in 1908, she made her first jump from a hot-air balloon and began touring with Charles Broadwick's World Famous Aeronauts. Mr. Broadwick legally adopted Tiny so it would be deemed proper for her to travel with him.

Tiny, age twenty, became the first woman to parachute from an airplane in 1913. She "created" the ripcord one year later. In 1922, after fourteen years of jumping over 1,100 times from balloons and airplanes, she retired at the age of twenty-nine years. She didn't want to, but her ankles had absorbed so much hurt and stress, they couldn't take any more.

For decades, the accomplishments of a young woman in an aviation world heavily dominated by men disappeared into obscurity. During World War II, Tiny worked for an aircraft company that produced airplane parts. She was asked as "the best in the business" to talk to young paratroopers about her experiences and to look at new parachute designs as they were developed. After the war, she lived an uneventful life for many years in southern California.

Her life took a sudden turn when she met Jim and Maxine Hix, a couple who were involved in aviation and had heard of Tiny's many brave accomplishments. They began inviting her to aviation group meetings, and soon Tiny was back in the aviation world where she belonged.

Photos Courtesy of The State Archives of North Carolina

In 1953, Tiny received the United States Government Pioneer Aviation Award on the fiftieth anniversary of the Wright brothers' first flight. She was given the John Glenn Medal in 1964 by the OX5 Club. In 1976, Tiny was inducted into the OX5 Hall of Fame along with Charles Lindbergh, Glenn Martin, and Orville and Wilbur Wright. She became one of the few female members of the Early Birds of Aviation. Her name was listed in *Who's Who in Aviation* and *The Guinness Book of World Records*.

Tiny died in 1978 at the age of eighty-five. In 1976, she had been made an honorary member of the 82nd Airborne Division from Fort Bragg. The Golden Knights parachuting team from the 82nd served as her pallbearers. On her tombstone are engraved the words First Lady of Parachuting.

Miss Tiny Broadwick
of The Broadwicks
World's Famous Aeronauts

SELECTED BIBLIOGRAPHY

"Georgia 'Tiny' Broadwick's Parachute." Smithsonian National Air and Space Museum, March 12, 2015, airandspace.si.edu/stories/editorial/georgia-%E2%80%9Ctiny%E2%80%9D-broadwicks-parachute.

Glessner, Bonnie. "Girl's Courage Sets New Mark." *Los Angeles Times*, January 10, 1914, newspapers.com/image/380153499.

Goerch, Carl. "She Made Over 1,100 Jumps." *The State Magazine*, December 1, 1945.

Poynter, Dan. "Tiny Broadwick." *Slideshare*, October 19, 2012, slideshare.net/Dan_Poynter/s-13-tiny-broadwick.

Ritter, Lisa. "Pack Man: Charles Broadwick Invented a New Way of Falling." *Air and Space Magazine*, May 2010.

Roberson, Elizabeth W. *Tiny Broadwick: The First Lady of Parachuting*. Gretna, LA: Pelican Publishing Company, 2001.

State Archives of North Carolina. *Tiny Broadwick Pioneer of Aviation Biography*. Raleigh, NC, files.nc.gov/dncr-archives/documents/files/tinybroadwick_bio.pdf.